To.. Pat
Love + Best Wishes
From.. John + Liz xx

Friendship, a clear balm...
A smile among dark frowns;
a beloved light
A solitude, a refuge, a delight

OTHER MINI GIFTBOOKS IN THIS SERIES:

Welcome to the New Baby
To a very special Aunt
To a very special Daughter
To a very special Grandmother
To a very special Mother-in-law
To a very special Grandpa
Happy Anniversary
To my very special Love
To a very special Mother
To a very special Son
To a very special Dad

To a very special Friend
To a very special Granddaughter
Wishing you Happiness
To my very special Husband
Merry Christmas
To a very special Sister
To my very special Wife
To someone special Happy
    Birthday
Wishing You The Best Birthday
    Ever

Published simultaneously in 1998 by Exley Publications LLC in the
USA and Exley Publications Ltd in Great Britain.

12 11 10 9 8 7 6 5 4 3 2 1

Copyright © Helen Exley 1998
ISBN 1-85015-932-7

A copy of the CIP data is available from the British Library on request.

Edited and words selected by Helen Exley
Illustrated by Juliette Clarke
Printed and bound in Hungary

Exley Publications Ltd, 16 Chalk Hill, Watford, Herts WD1 4BN, UK.
Exley Publications LLC, 232 Madison Avenue, Suite 1206,
NY 10016, USA.

ACKNOWLEDGEMENTS: The publishers are grateful for permission to reproduce copyright
material. Whilst every reasonable effort has been made to trace copyright holders, the
publishers would be pleased to hear from any not here acknowledged. PABLO CASALS: from
Joys and Sorrows, published by Little, Brown UK. PO CHU-I: From "On Being 60", from
Chinese Poems, translated by Arthur Waley. Published by HarperCollins Publishers Ltd. T.S.
ELIOT: From Time, October 1950. GEORGE SANTAYANA: From My Host The World, from
Persons and Places, 1953, published by MIT Press. Pam Brown, Pamela Dugdale, Helen Exley,
Charlotte Gray and Helen Thomson © 1998.

To someone very special

HAPPY BIRTHDAY

Edited by Helen Exley
Illustrated by Juliette Clarke

Here's wishing you
a long and rewarding life.
Have a happy day and
a *great* year ahead!

. . .

A HELEN EXLEY GIFTBOOK

EXLEY
NEW YORK • WATFORD, UK

HAPPY BIRTHDAY!

Today we wish you laughter and song and silliness – and people who love you and people you love all about you, sharing your happiness.

Yes, birthdays are times for looking back and looking forward – in between drinks and cake and balloons and laughter.

PAM BROWN, b.1928

. . .

I wish you, every birthday, some new love of lovely things, and some new forgetfulness of the teasing things, and some higher pride in the praising things, and some sweeter peace from the hurrying things and some closer fence from the worrying things. And longer stay of time when you are happy and lighter flight of days that are unkind.

JOHN RUSKIN (1819-1900)

…

Pleas'd to look forward, pleas'd to look behind, and count each Birthday with a grateful mind.

ALEXANDER POPE (1688-1744)

…

I am an old man, but in many senses a very young man. And this is what I want you to be – young, young all your life, and to say things to the world that are true.

PABLO CASALS (1876-1973)

…

LIVE LIFE TO THE FULL

After sixty, who on earth counts
birthdays?
You can't start again at sixty
– but you can make jolly good use of what
you've got.

PAM BROWN, b.1928

. . .

It matters not how long you live, but how well.

PUBLILIUS SYRUS

. . .

Nobody ever gets far in life if they
walk backward.
The best lies ahead of you.

CHARLOTTE GRAY, b.1937

. . .

Live all you can; it's a mistake not to.
It doesn't so much matter what you do in particular
so long as you have your life.

HENRY JAMES (1843-1916)

...

The only thing I regret about my past is the length
of it. If I had my past life over again, I'd make all
the same mistakes – only sooner.

TALLULAH BANKHEAD (1903-1968),
FROM "THE TIMES", JULY 28, 1981

...

I still want to do my work, I still want to do my
livingness. And I have lived. I have been fulfilled.
I recognized what I had, and I never sold it short.
And I ain't through yet!

LOUISE NEVELSON, b.1899

...

YOU SURE KNOW WHEN
YOU'RE OVER 60!

You know you're getting old

when you stoop to tie your shoes and wonder

what else you can do while you're

down there.

GEORGE BURNS

...

Sixty is... when you pull a funny face and you look a lot better.

HELEN EXLEY

...

Being over sixty is when you keep your old elegance – but it doesn't show.
Sixty is when you pull yourself up in the way that once made you look like a fashion model – and nothing happens at all.
Sixty is when you realize the bus driver sees you as a daft old wreck.
Sixty is when it's essential to keep your tongue sharp – in order to run through condescending little officials.

PAMELA DUGDALE

...

You're getting beyond it when putting on five pounds disguises your wrinkles.

HELEN THOMSON, b.1943

For the unlearned,
old age is
winter; for the
learned, it is
the season
of the harvest.

HASIDIC SAYING

…

LEARNING, LIVING

Learn – for as long as you learn you're alive!
Live – for as long as you live you can learn!

PAM BROWN, b.1928

…

I never feel age…. If you have creative work, you
don't have age or time.

LOUISE NEVELSON, b.1899

Do not say, "It is morning," and dismiss it with a name of yesterday. See it for the first time as a newborn child that has no name.

RABINDRANATH TAGORE (1861-1941)

...

The world grows more complex.
Things change with ever increasing speed.
Good.
Enquire. Investigate. Discover.
While the mind is curious it is alive and kicking.

PAMELA DUGDALE

...

I promise to keep on living as though I expected to live forever. Nobody grows old by merely living a number of years. People grow old only by deserting their ideals. Years may wrinkle the skin, but to give up interest wrinkles the soul.

DOUGLAS MACARTHUR (1880-1964)

...

ALL DISINTEGRATING TOGETHER!

Friends who are contemporaries and
of long acquaintance fall apart at more
or less the same speed. And so, the
aches and creaks and wheezes that
come with age are transferred into
companionable things – symptoms to swap,
disintegrations to chart with a certain
dry amusement.
For how ridiculous it is that we, who only
a flicker of time ago were young and very
nearly beautiful, have come to this.
Only friends, gossiping over a cup of tea, can
see the joke... knowing that, beneath the skin,
we have not changed a scrap.

PAM BROWN, b.1928

...

NO OBJECTS OF VALUE... ARE WORTH RISKING

THE PRICELESS EXPERIENCE

OF WAKING UP ONE MORE DAY.

JACK SMITH

...

CELEBRATE LIFE!

I like living. I have sometimes been wildly,

despairingly, acutely miserable,

racked with sorrow, but through it all I

still know quite certainly

that just to be alive is a grand thing.

AGATHA CHRISTIE (1890-1976)

...

For the past eighty years I have started each
day in the same manner. It is not a
mechanical routine but something essential
to my daily life. I go to the piano, and
I play two preludes and fugues of Bach. I cannot
think of doing otherwise. It is a sort
of benediction on the house. But that is not
its only meaning for me. It is a
rediscovery of the world of which I have
the joy of being a part.
It fills me with awareness of the wonder of
life, with a feeling of the
incredible marvel of being a human being.

PABLO CASALS (1876-1973)
FROM "JOYS AND SORROWS"

. . .

I used to trouble about what life was for – now
being alive seems sufficient reason.

JOANNA FIELD

. . .

<u>OLD WRECKS ANONYMOUS!</u>

How is it that when I'd planned to be

thin and elegant

and white haired in old age – I'm stout and fat

and a washed-out ginger?

PAM BROWN, b.1928

...

Age seldom arrives smoothly or quickly. It's more often a succession of jerks.

JEAN RHYS (1894-1979)

. . .

I must be getting absent-minded. Whenever I complain that things aren't what they used to be, I always forget to include myself.

GEORGE BURNS

. . .

The years between fifty and seventy are the hardest. You are always being asked to do things, and you are not yet decrepit enough to turn them down.

T.S. ELIOT (1888-1965)

. . .

Old people shouldn't eat health foods. They need all the preservatives they can get.

ROBERT ORBEN

. . .

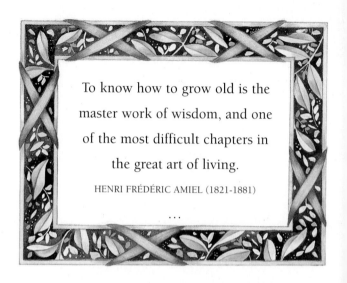

To know how to grow old is the master work of wisdom, and one of the most difficult chapters in the great art of living.

HENRI FRÉDÉRIC AMIEL (1821-1881)

...

ACCEPTANCE, CONTENTMENT

It was formerly a terrifying view to me that I should one day be an old woman. I now find that Nature has provided pleasures for every state.

LADY MARY WORTLEY MONTAGU (1689-1762)

...

That is the mystery of grace: it never comes too late.

FRANÇOIS MAURIAC

...

In youth, everything seems possible; but we reach a point in the middle years when we realize that we are never going to reach all the shining goals we had set for ourselves. And in the end, most of us reconcile ourselves, with what grace we can, to living with our ulcers and arthritis, our sense of partial failure, our less-than-ideal families – and even our politicians!

ADLAI E. STEVENSON (1900-1965)

. . .

Childhood must pass away, and then youth, as surely as age approaches. The true wisdom is to be always seasonable, and to change with good grace in changing circumstances. To love playthings well as a child, to lead an adventurous and honourable youth, and to settle when the time arrives, into a green and smiling age....

ROBERT LOUIS STEVENSON (1850-1894)

. . .

FEELING YOUNGER EVERY DAY

You can't help getting older,
but you don't have to get old.

GEORGE BURNS

. . .

To be seventy years young is
sometimes far
more cheerful and hopeful than
to be forty years old.

OLIVER WENDELL HOLMES (1809-1894)

. . .

Whether seventy or sixteen,
there can be in
every being's heart the love of
wonder... the unfailing childlike
appetite for what is next,
and a joy of the game of life.

SAMUEL ULLMAN

. . .

There is a fountain of youth: it is
your mind, your talents, the
creativity you bring to your life and
the lives of people you love.
When you learn to tap this source,
you will have truly defeated age.

SOPHIA LOREN, b.1934

· · ·

I was born old and get younger
every day. At present I am
sixty years young.

HERBERT BEERBOHM TREE (1853-1917)

· · ·

It takes a long time to become
young.

PABLO PICASSO (1881-1973)

· · ·

THE QUIET YEARS

I am enjoying to the
full that period of reflection which is the
happiest conclusion to a life of action.

WILLA CATHER (1876-1947)

. . .

What I ought to do.

Simplify. Stop bothering with the non-essentials. Having devoted my life to my work so far, I should reap the harvest and learn how to live the rest of it properly. You can be lazy at last, so enjoy yourself, man. It's time now for trees and grass and growing things. You've nothing to be ashamed of on your road so far, you've done your best for your work and for the public. So now be content, settle down and concentrate on playing the last act gracefully.

MAURICE CHEVALIER (1888-1972)

. . .

... from fifty to sixty one is free from all ills;
Calm and still – the heart enjoys rest.
I have put behind me Love and Greed, I have done with Profit and Fame.... Still my heart has spirit enough to listen to flutes and strings. At leisure I open new wine and taste several cups....

PO CHU-I (772-846)

. . .

A STRANGE BEAUTY IN AGE

As we grow old, the beauty steals inward.

RALPH WALDO EMERSON (1803-1882)

...

When grace is joined with wrinkles it is
adorable. There is an unspeakable dawn in
happy old age.

VICTOR HUGO (1802-1885)

...

The rhythms of the dance change
with time
– but still hold power and beauty.

PAM BROWN, b.1928

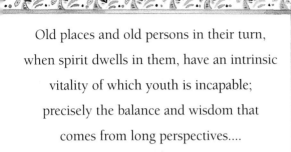

Old places and old persons in their turn,
when spirit dwells in them, have an intrinsic
vitality of which youth is incapable;
precisely the balance and wisdom that
comes from long perspectives....

GEORGE SANTAYANA, FROM "MY HOST THE WORLD"

...

You know, you can only perceive real
beauty in a person as they get older.

ANOUK AIMEE, b.1932

...

The evening star is the most beautiful
of all stars.

SAPPHO

BIRTHDAY TOASTS

May you always find new projects, new friends,

new love.

May you always find new paths to wander, new

adventures to dare,

new chapters of life to open,

new changes to challenge you.

HELEN THOMSON, b.1943

May the years be kind. May every hardship give you greater strength, and every sadness be crowned with greater joy.

PAM BROWN, b.1928

...

May the road rise up to meet you. May the wind be always at your back.
May the sun shine warm upon your face and the rain fall safe upon your head, and... may God hold you in the palm of his hand.

AUTHOR UNKNOWN

...

May your age be as old as a mountain and your happiness as deep as the sea.

IRISH TOAST

...

To your good health, old friend, may you live for a thousand years, and I be there to count them.

ROBERT SMITH SURTEES (1803-1864)